GETTING THE
MESSAGE

Television
and Radio

How to interpret
what we see, read and hear

Sean Connolly

FRANKLIN WATTS
LONDON • SYDNEY

 An Appleseed Editions book

First published in 2009 by Franklin Watts
338 Euston Road, London NW1 3BH

Franklin Watts Australia
Hachette Children's Books
Level 17/207 Kent St, Sydney, NSW 2000

© 2009 Appleseed Editions

Created by Appleseed Editions Ltd,
Well House, Friars Hill, Guestling,
East Sussex TN35 4ET

Designed by Helen James
Edited by Mary-Jane Wilkins
Picture research by Su Alexander

ISBN 978 0 7496 8783 0

Dewey Classification: 302.23' 4

A CIP catalogue for this book is available from the British Library.

Photograph acknowledgements
page 6 Christopher Farina/Corbis; 9 ClassicStock/Alamy; 11 Bettmann/Corbis;
12 Sarah Rice/Star Ledger/Corbis; 14 top Julio Etchart/Alamy, bottom ClassicStock/Alamy;
16 Naval Historical Foundation; 18 BBC/Corbis; 20 Content Mine International/Alamy;
22 & 24 Getty Images; 27 Lucas Jackson/Reuters/Corbis; 28 Mary Evans Picture Library/
Alamy; 30 Robert Galbraith/Reuters/Corbis; 32 Corbis; 35 Bettmann/Corbis; 36 Getty
Images; 38 Vario Images GmbH & Co.KG/Alamy; 40 Sam Diephuis/Zefa/Corbis
Front cover Christopher Farina/Corbis

Printed in China

Franklin Watts is a division of Hachette Children's Books,
an Hachette UK company.
www.hachette.co.uk

Contents

The power of broadcasting

Try this: count up all the television sets and radios in your house and then work out how many your parents had in their home when they were your age. Unless you live on a desert island, today's number will be much greater than it was 25 or 30 years ago. Then try to find out whether your grandparents or great-grandparents had television and radio sets.

A visitor examines the new generation, flat-screen televisions on display at an electronics exhibition in Las Vegas.

This comparison tells us a great deal about how people received information and were entertained in the past. People are naturally curious and have always found ways of sending and receiving information and news – by word of mouth (including town criers), or through newspapers, magazines or letters. Each of these media works on a limited scale: one-to-one, in a town or across a larger region.

The electronic era

Television and radio are also media, but they have a much greater range than the media that came before them. In fact, their range is global, because they are based on electronic technology. Today we often use the term media (rather than electronic media) to describe television and radio, and older media are known as traditional media.

Television and radio are so widespread and popular that they have the power to affect nearly every aspect of how we live: what we buy, how we eat, what we wear and even when we go to war. With this power comes responsibility – for those providing the information as well as for those receiving it. This book examines how both sides of this equation do their job. The producers of the programmes we see and hear on TV and radio must follow guidelines about fairness and accuracy. Otherwise, they could misuse their power. Most societies ensure that these guidelines are drawn up and monitored closely (see pages 37-39).

Perhaps more important, though, is people's responsibility to understand the information that is sent out 24 hours a day. This understanding is called media literacy. Traditional literacy taught in schools emphasizes the importance of the skills of reading and writing. Ofcom (see page 39) describes media literacy as 'the ability to access, understand and create communications in a variety of contexts'. That definition might seem a little dry, but it neatly captures the skills that we all need to develop if we are to keep pace with what the constantly changing world of television and radio offers us.

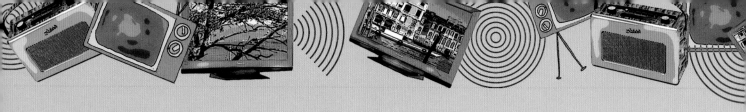

The broadcast era

Most people feel let down if they tell a friend some news, only to be told it's ancient history or that the friend thinks something else is the real news. It's human nature to want to know about what is happening around us – and in the wider world – as soon as possible. Television and radio tell us just that, and they also bring us hugely popular forms of entertainment and education.

Following a tradition

Throughout history, people have sent information from one place to another as fast as they could. Receiving news quickly satisfies people's curiosity, but it can also make a difference to important conflicts. Legend has it that the messenger Pheidippides brought news of a Greek victory over the Persians in 490BC by running all the way from the battlefield at Marathon to Athens. The news boosted Greek morale, and helped them overcome the Persian invasion. If it had taken longer to arrive, the Greeks might have assumed that their soldiers had lost the battle and fled.

Light travels many thousands of times faster than any human, so the Greeks and other ancient people built signal beacons to act as warnings of invasions. By placing a string of beacons so that each beacon is just visible on the horizon from the previous one, defenders could send warnings over long distances in very little time (just the time it took to light each hilltop bonfire). Archaeologists believe that only six signals covered the whole 240-km length of Offa's Dyke, dividing Wales from England in early medieval times.

The nineteenth century saw the first real communications breakthrough, enabling people to send detailed messages far more quickly. The arrival of trains was the first boost, but the real revolution came with the

Many families in the 1940s spent their evenings gathered around the radio listening to programmes together.

development of the telegraph in the 1830s. Messages could be sent along electric wires, arriving instantly at their destination. Long cables eventually crossed continents and even oceans by the end of the century.

In 1897, the Italian inventor Guglielmo Marconi demonstrated that the same signals could be sent without wires, using radio signals. Within ten years, radio operators were sending and receiving all sorts of sounds, including music and the human voice. Modern radio was born. Over the next few decades inventors pioneered ways of sending images as well as sounds – through television systems. John Logie Baird demonstrated the first workable television system in London in 1925, but it was more than 20 years before television became a widespread form of broadcasting.

Into the home

During the first half of the twentieth century listening to the radio was a family affair: everyone sat quietly as favourite comedies, variety programmes or news reports were broadcast. Singers, musicians, comedians and actors became famous overnight through performing on some of these popular programmes.

Politicians soon learned the importance of having such an attentive audience. Winston Churchill, the British prime minister throughout the Second World War, used the radio to raise British wartime morale and to stir the British public into making further sacrifices for the war effort. One of his most important – and influential – radio addresses was broadcast on 18 June 1940.

Adolf Hitler's German soldiers had just forced the French to surrender and everyone believed he would turn his sights on Britain next. Churchill's speech was a call to arms, especially in passages such as this. 'The whole fury and might of the enemy must very soon be turned on us. Hitler knows that he will have to break us in this island or lose the war. If we can stand up to him, all Europe may be freed and the life of the world may move forward into broad, sunlit uplands.'

Television took over from radio as the most popular form of broadcasting after the war. Families gathered around the television set, which was one of the largest and most expensive pieces of furniture in the house. Some early television programmes look stiff and old-fashioned now, but much of today's programming was inspired by ideas first aired more than 50 years ago. Viewers watched TV chefs such as Marguerite Patten and Fanny Cradock. Chat shows, sporting fixtures and even the Eurovision Song Contest all have long histories on television.

Out and about

Television and radio have broken free of the indoor limitations of the past – recording studios for broadcasting and sitting rooms for audiences. Outside broadcasting, using mobile cameras and sound equipment, takes audiences right to the heart of events as they happen. Whether they are looking at fish living hundreds of metres beneath the sea or watching astronauts walking in space, people can now have an inside view of what could only be dreamt about years ago.

Similarly, audiences no longer need to be sitting at home to enjoy television and radio. Both are already forms of instant communication. New developments in both media have reduced costs and improved reception – almost anywhere people want to watch or listen.

The first TV quizzes – and scandals – began during the 1950s. Charles Van Doren (right) admitted that he had received answers from the producers of the American quiz show Twenty-one *in 1959.*

Tuning in

The term broadcasting now usually describes the media of television and radio, but the word originated on farms. A farmer would walk through a field, throwing (or casting) seeds as widely (broadly) as possible to ensure that the whole field was sowed with seed. The farmer was broadcasting his seeds.

Elvis Duran (left) broadcasts his popular Morning Zoo *programme live to radio audiences in New York City, Pennsylvania, Ohio and Florida every day.*

Radio and television stations broadcast signals all around them in the same way, reaching everywhere within a particular range. Traditional broadcasting systems send out these audio or video signals from stations, going first from a transmitter to an aerial that is usually on top of the building. The signal reaches the listener or viewer through a receiver in the radio or television, which can convert the signal into either sounds or images. This system works well for people living close to cities with TV and radio stations. The sound quality and television images are clear. But reception grows worse

SPOTLIGHT ON
Signalling change

Broadcasting is changing fast. Many homes receive television signals through wires or from satellites orbiting the Earth. Cable television sends a signal along a line, and each television is plugged into a branch of the line. This system guarantees the same clear image all along the line – the image does not fade at a distance from the source of the signal, in the way traditional broadcast signals do. To receive satellite television households need to install a satellite dish which receives signals bounced back to Earth from a broadcasting satellite.

Both systems are only available if viewers pay an extra fee, which covers the cost of the cable or the satellite system. In return, viewers receive dozens or even hundreds of channels. Some channels – for new films or special sporting events, for example – are scrambled. Viewers can only watch if they pay an extra fee. Other TV and radio systems are in the pipeline (see pages 40-43).

No matter how people receive television or radio broadcasts, video and audio signals are increasingly sent using a digital system. The main advantages of digital over the older system (called analogue) are the clear quality of sounds and images and the wide choice of programmes. All broadcasting will be digital within a few years. In the meantime, older televisions can receive digital broadcasts by adding a special box which receives digital signals to the set and hooking it up.

An array of satellite dishes on the BBC Television Centre in London picks up signals from around the world. Transmitters inside the building then re-broadcast these signals to televisions in Britain.

Right: televisions in the 1950s needed V-shaped aerials (nicknamed rabbit ears) in order to produce a clear picture on the screen.

at greater distances unless boosters strengthen the signals for people living in more remote regions. It is costly to build such boosters in remote or mountainous areas. Modern broadcasting methods (see Spotlight on page 13) offer people in these regions a chance to see – and hear – what they might otherwise miss.

Spreading the message

Broadcasting involves sending a signal out in all directions, so it is possible to reach an enormous area with the same message. A system of broadcasting which uses boosters is called a network. The word network usually describes natural connections, such as the network of veins and arteries carrying blood to all parts of our bodies.

A broadcasting network also delivers something – in this case a radio or TV signal – to all parts of a region or country. It is expensive to build all the transmitters and signal boosters needed to set up a national network. As a result, the money to run a broadcasting network must come from either the people who use it, or from private companies which make their money from advertising (see pages 16-19).

GIANTS IN THE SKY

SOME PEOPLE BELIEVE THAT SATELLITE BROADCASTING COMPANIES SHOULD BE MORE CLOSELY CONTROLLED. IF A SATELLITE BROADCASTER ALREADY OWNS MEDIA COMPANIES SUCH AS DAILY NEWSPAPERS SHOULD IT BE ALLOWED TO OWN A TELEVISION STATION AS WELL? THE FEAR IS THAT THE BROADCASTER MIGHT USE ITS INFLUENCE TO STIFLE UNFAVOURABLE NEWS REPORTS. OTHERS DEFEND BROADCASTERS, SAYING THAT THEY SPEND A LOT OF MONEY TO PROVIDE A PUBLIC SERVICE SO GOVERNMENTS SHOULD NOT INTERFERE. WHAT DO YOU THINK?

Sending a signal

Wireless radio was an important development in the early twentieth century. One of the first industries to benefit was shipping. Some countries passed laws forcing commercial ships to have a radio transmitter and an operator trained to use it on board. This was so that ships in distress could use radio communications to help rescue efforts. Before they had radio links, ships relied on flags or signal flares to summon help. Radios could send distress calls much further, and operated in all sorts of weather.

The shipping industry also paved the way for setting up the first broadcasting network. In 1904, the United Fruit Company hired American inventor Lee de Forest to set up a chain of radio broadcasting stations between Central America and the United States. Ships carrying the company's bananas and other tropical fruits relied on these stations for information about weather and prices.

The commercial route

The United Fruit Company operation provided radio communication far beyond the range of a single transmitter, but in other ways it was very different from modern broadcast networks. For example, its audience – the company's ships – was deliberately limited. Also, the programmes had nothing to do with entertainment.

Opposite: a United Fruit Company ship off the coast of Central America in the early twentieth century. Transporting bananas and other tropical fruits to US ports was big business, so the company built a radio network to help ships navigate quickly and safely.

In one important way, this pioneering radio network set an example that other American networks followed: it was set up to help a company make more money. American broadcasting, from its earliest radio networks to today's multimedia giants, is dominated by large commercial companies.

The first radio stations which broadcast regular programmes to the public were begun by American radio manufacturers in the early 1920s. Their aim was to encourage people to buy radios. They succeeded dramatically – in 1922, fewer than 60,000 American homes had radios, but by 1929 the number had risen to ten million. Along the way, the radio manufacturers found that other companies were prepared to pay for air time to broadcast radio advertising, or commercials.

An important pattern was set. The National Broadcasting Company, set up in 1926, was developed as a network of radio stations broadcasting across the United States. The network earned income from commercials, and companies advertised on programmes relevant to the products they sold. For example, laundry soap makers chose to advertise on romantic dramas that appealed to American women. People nicknamed these programmes soap operas.

John Reith, the first BBC director-general, locks up the BBC headquarters after the last programme one evening in May 1932. Reith had strong views about the BBC and its mission, and his influence is still felt today.

This commercial arrangement, in which advertising paid for the enormous network costs, is still in place today. Although America does have a public (non-commercial) broadcasting network, most Americans watch and listen to commercial television and radio.

The public good

Broadcasting in Britain started as it did in the US, when a group of radio manufacturers set up the British Broadcasting Company in 1922. In 1926, this company became a national network called the British Broadcasting Corporation (BBC). Unlike American networks, the BBC was a non-commercial organization from the start. Instead of earning money through advertising, it received money from the public, through an annual licence fee that all radio-owning households had to pay.

The first director-general of the BBC, Lord Reith, was proud that the corporation was free of both commercial influence and direct political control. He believed that radio had a duty to educate and improve the lives of people. When supporters of the BBC fear that it might introduce advertising or change its way of operating, they often refer to Lord Reith's own description of the aims of the BBC. He used a Latin phrase: *edocere, erudire, delectare*, or 'to educate, inform and entertain'.

SPOTLIGHT ON

Paying for the BBC

The BBC prides itself on being free of both government control and the influence of advertisers. This is because it receives money every year from a licence fee that every household which has a television has to buy. A TV licence costs about £140 (less for blind people and free for the elderly). The BBC spends this money on eight TV channels, ten radio networks, more than 50 local TV and radio services, and the World Service, which provides foreign audiences with information about the UK.

THE JOKE THAT BACKFIRED

ON 18 OCTOBER 2008, COMEDIAN RUSSELL BRAND AND BROADCASTER JONATHAN ROSS LEFT A SERIES OF RUDE MESSAGES ON THE ANSWERING MACHINE OF ANDREW SACHS. SACHS IS ONE OF BRITAIN'S BEST-LOVED COMEDY ACTORS. RECORDINGS OF THE MESSAGES WERE BROADCAST LATER THAT DAY, ON BRAND'S BBC RADIO 2 PROGRAMME.

ONLY TWO LISTENERS COMPLAINED ABOUT THE STUNT ON THE DAY, BUT NEWSPAPERS REPORTED IT, DEMANDING THAT THE BBC TAKE ACTION. THE OUTCRY GREW UNTIL THE BBC SUSPENDED THE PAIR. BRAND THEN RESIGNED, AND THE BBC SUSPENDED ROSS FOR 12 WEEKS WITHOUT PAY. LESLEY DOUGLAS, CONTROLLER OF RADIO 2, RESIGNED THE FOLLOWING DAY.

HOW DO YOU THINK THE BBC SHOULD HAVE DEALT WITH THIS JOKE THAT BACKFIRED?

Over to YOU

Aiming for an audience

People make their own choices about which programmes they listen to or watch – and for how long. Programme-makers and broadcasting networks pay close attention to the choices audiences make. Sometimes they can encourage audiences to watch programmes that were not very popular when they were first broadcast.

The BBC comedy *The Office*, for example, was initially watched by small audiences, but gained popularity as television critics agreed on how good it was and word-of-mouth recommendations spread. The BBC could have dropped the programme after poor early ratings (see page 25). Instead, it waited for viewers to hear about and start watching the programme.

Despite being set in a typical American town, The Simpsons has become one of the most popular television programmes in the world. Its jokes work on several levels, so it attracts viewers from all age groups.

Broadcasting networks need to make programmes that appeal to the different groups that make up an overall audience. Daytime television, for example, has traditionally been aimed at young children and their mothers. Sport dominates much of the weekend on both radio and television. Most religious programmes are aired on Sundays.

Occasionally, a very successful programme crosses these boundaries and becomes very popular with wide audiences. Children and adults alike enjoy *The Simpsons*, although the two groups enjoy episodes for different reasons. The children enjoy the slapstick and the silliness of the Simpson family, while their parents appreciate the satire that the programme's writers weave into each episode.

There are more TV channels and radio stations today than ever before, and many are aimed at specific audiences. So it becomes harder for a single programme to appeal to different audiences. This might not be a problem in itself. For example, a beer company might advertise on a sport or car programme even if few women watch it – so long as young men tune in. And if far more women watch a programme devoted to fashion, then a lipstick-maker will be happy to advertise on it.

The pirates

Sometimes unlicensed radio broadcasters set up pirate radio stations. These stations first became popular during the 1960s, when Britain had very few radio stations which played pop music. Pirate stations such as Radio Caroline operated from ships anchored in international waters (outside British boundaries), beaming programmes to UK listeners. As more and more British radio stations were launched, the need for pirate stations lessened and they shut down.

More recently, a new brand of inner-city pirate station has cropped up, pumping out dance music from flats and using transmitters on rooftops. About 150 of these illegal stations operate in the UK, half of them in or around London. Pirate radio operators risk being fined or being given criminal sentences because their illegal transmitters can block emergency-service radio contact (see Talking heads).

Long-term effects

Audience viewing figures affect which programmes are made: by and large, popular programmes continue to run year after year, while unpopular ones are soon cancelled. But what about the opposite process? How does broadcasting affect audiences?

Social observers and educational experts – as well as many parents – wonder what effect broadcasting (especially television) has over a long period. Does watching lots of television at home help or hinder children's performance at school? Does it have any effect on the time people spend on other activities such as reading for pleasure? Do young people who watch a lot of television think or behave in ways that are recognizable?

Staff and disc jockeys from Radio Caroline prepare to leave the ship at the port of Felixstowe after the government passed laws that forced the station to close in 1967.

Scientists have examined all these subjects and come up with some interesting conclusions. British people are particularly interested in the results because studies have shown that people in the UK spend 18 hours a week watching television – more than viewers in any other European country. The results, however, paint a confused picture. Some suggest that schoolwork and reading for pleasure do suffer because homework and reading seem too challenging compared with watching television. Others, however, indicate that maths and literacy skills might improve if children watch more television because some programmes help young people develop learning skills.

A survey of children aged between six and nine published in 2008 found that children who were read to at least three times a week and whose parents discussed television programmes with them spent less time watching television than other children and also did better at school. Probably watching television is just one factor which can affect achievements along with which programmes children choose to watch and their family lives and circumstances.

TALKING HEADS

PIRATE RADIO

Many people consider pirate radio stations to be cheeky and daring – and good fun. That might have been true of the radio ships of the 1960s, but modern pirate stations can be very dangerous. Terry Stacy of London's Islington Council spells out some of the risks: 'Illegal broadcasters can put lives at risk by interfering with vital emergency equipment, damage council property and make the lives of our residents hell. Sometimes these stations are linked to drug-dealing and serious crime, which we will not tolerate.'

The right message

The core of any medium – radio or television, newspaper or magazine – is the message being sent out. We need to understand not just what is being said on a particular radio station or television network, but why it is being said. And the message can change over time. Again, people need to be aware of how and why that happens.

SPOTLIGHT ON

Ratings

Broadcasters in most countries keep an eye on how many people listen to a particular radio station or watch a TV programme. Companies specialize in supplying this information, called programme ratings. Commercial networks need to make sure their programmes are popular enough to attract advertisers. Non-commercial networks may face harsher critics – the viewers. The BBC knows that audiences will complain if they believe that money from their licence fee (see page 19) is being wasted on unpopular programmes.

Working out ratings – what people watch or listen to at a particular time – calls for special skills. It would be impossible to ask every household in the country. Instead, a cross section of homes is selected in which

small transmitters are hooked up to their radios and televisions. These homes represent a mini-version of the country as a whole. For example, if 25 per cent of the national population live in or around London, then 25 per cent of the selected homes will also be there. If 12 per cent live in Scotland, then 12 per cent of the ratings households will be Scottish, and so on.

Broadcasters can find all sorts of answers from the ratings information coming from these homes. They can even work out whether a programme is popular or unpopular while it is being watched. After studying the ratings, they can decide whether to pump more money into making certain programmes, or to pull the plug when the series ends.

Changing attitudes

Apart from countries ruled by dictators, where broadcasters are strictly controlled by the government, most societies expect television and radio to be fair and free. The fairness is often judged by how news stories are presented. A truly free system allows news programmes to criticize the government or, in the case of privately-owned broadcasting, the network owners themselves. Other programmes can take a critical stand: *The Simpsons*, for example, often pokes fun at the Fox television network which produces the series. Viewers judge

Opposite: African-Americans and other groups believe that ratings-gathering companies such as Nielsen ignore their viewing preferences.

COMMUNITY VOICE

The actor and writer Kulvinder Ghir has worked on several British TV comedies since the early 1990s. He has seen attitudes to race change on both sides of the camera during that time. As a non-white British actor, he is aware of the problems faced by the writers and cast of *The Real McCoys*, a programme set in Britain's Afro-Caribbean community:

'After every sketch, there'd be a big discussion about whether it presented the black community in a positive light. They wouldn't do a sketch involving a bank robber because they didn't want to portray black people as bank robbers, even though everybody else in the sketch was black as well. In terms of comedy, that's very limiting.'

In that series, Ghir felt that because he wasn't Afro-Caribbean himself, he could not be as free to decide what to include. Several years later he was involved with *Goodness Gracious Me*, an extremely popular comedy set in Britain's Asian community. Ghir and others with an Asian background had more freedom to influence that series:

'When we first did it we had no idea it was going to be successful and it wasn't a preplanned thing of what would work and what wouldn't. I think it was successful because it came from us. We dug deep into our culture and celebrated it. We dealt with the simple issue of humanity. I think that when you balance culture with humanity, nobody is that much different from anybody else and that's what made the series mainstream.'

fairness according to how different parts of society are presented. For example, people would be outraged today if a new TV series constantly targeted a particular racial group, or gay people, or citizens with disabilities. But 20 or 30 years ago, programme-makers felt that such groups were fair game for mockery – if anyone complained, they

were accused of lacking a sense of humour or of stirring up trouble. So broadcasters need to balance their freedom to produce the programmes they choose to and the effect this freedom might have.

The BBC felt some of the same pressures during the prank phone call crisis in late 2008 (see page 19). Many people – including prime minister Gordon Brown and opposition leader David Cameron – were shocked that the publicly-funded BBC could behave cruelly towards a popular old man. Others claimed that any punishment would limit the BBC's freedom to produce edgy comedy in the future.

Comedian Graham Norton is popular on both sides of the Atlantic. Twenty years ago, his openness about being gay might have damaged his career.

Over to YOU

ROLE MODELS OR FIGURES OF FUN?

DURING THE 1970S AND 1980S, MANY AMERICAN TELEVISION PROGRAMMES INCLUDED BLACK CHARACTERS IN ROLES OF AUTHORITY – AS DOCTORS, TEACHERS, JUDGES AND SO ON – AND USED BLACK ACTORS RATHER LESS IN THE ROLE OF VILLAINS. SUPPORTERS OF THIS TREND ARGUED THAT THE RESPONSIBLE CHARACTERS ON TV SCREENS PROVIDED ROLE MODELS FOR YOUNG BLACK PEOPLE AND AT THE SAME TIME HELPED WHITE PEOPLE OVERCOME SOME OF THEIR PREJUDICES. OTHERS DISAGREED, SAYING THAT AUDIENCES CONSIDER SUCH EFFORTS AS CLUMSY, CAUSING THEM TO STICK TO THEIR ATTITUDES. WHICH SIDE DO YOU THINK IS RIGHT IN THIS DEBATE?

Back to reality

On Halloween evening in 1938 American radio listeners had a shock. Millions had tuned into a programme of South American dance music broadcast live from a New York hotel. The music began as scheduled, but the programme was interrupted by news bulletins. The first announced that scientists had observed strange lights on the planet Mars. Later bulletins spoke of a disturbance in New Jersey, not far from New York. Before long, the music was abandoned and listeners began to hear terrifying reports of a crash site in New Jersey.

Broadcaster Orson Welles faced tough questions from reporters after his War of the Worlds prank in October 1938. He expressed deep regret, but must have known that his fame would grow as a result of the dramatic events.

SPOTLIGHT ON
Realism deficiency

Is reality TV harmless? Some people believe it can affect the way young people view the world and how they can succeed in it. In 2004, the *Times Educational Supplement* reported on a condition called Beckham syndrome, which some educational experts believe affects 40 per cent of British teenagers. These young people have a 'realism deficiency' which comes from watching too many reality TV programmes. They believe that success can come overnight – just as it does for the winners of *Pop Idol* and *Fame Academy* – rather than as a result of long hours spent studying.

It emerged that a spaceship from Mars had landed there, and that huge creatures were emerging from it, destroying everything in sight. Radio audiences heard terrifying shrieks and crashes along with tearful accounts by the reporters. Or did they?

The terrifying broadcast was actually a trick: the brilliant American actor and director Orson Welles had adapted the HG Wells science-fiction novel *War of the Worlds* about a Martian invasion. By treating it as if it were a news story, he made the novel seem real to listeners. Welles had warned listeners about what was to happen at the beginning of the programme, but many people ignored the warning or didn't hear it.

Modern versions

The events of that night more than 70 years ago began a discussion that is still going on today. Can we believe what we hear on the radio or see on the television? Should we? Is reality the same as truth? These are difficult questions, which involve everyone and are important for several reasons. The first is that radio and television can trick audiences into believing that they are hearing or seeing something that is not really there. Some of this trickery might be harmless, such as the image of the pretty girl singing at the

ACCURATE PREDICTION

The American artist Andy Warhol devoted much of his work to the effects of the mass media on society. His paintings often seem like frozen images from the television screen, or like the pictures that are repeated over and over on millions of T-shirts. Like other social observers, he saw how the media could turn almost anyone into a celebrity – and then just as quickly forget that same person. In 1968, he predicted: 'In the future, everyone will be world famous for fifteen minutes.' Eleven years later Warhol added: 'My prediction from the sixties finally came true: In the future, everyone will be famous for fifteen minutes.' Nowadays, in the age of reality television and 24-hour news, Warhol's observation seems more and more accurate.

Opposite: Fantasia Barrino (left) and Diana DeGarmo compete in the 2004 finals of American Idol. As with many reality television programmes, the viewers are the ultimate judges of the competition. Barrino was the series winner, and earned a valuable recording contract.

opening of the 2008 Olympics in China. It later emerged that she was not the real singer – she only moved her lips in time to the song. But she was chosen because the Chinese government believed that she was prettier than the real singer.

Many people believe that the broadcast media have played more serious tricks on the viewing public. In April 2008, the *New York Times* reported that the US Department of Defense had given special treatment to about a dozen military experts who often appear on American television. The result, according to the newspaper, was a big change in the way these experts described the actions of the US government: they were far more favourable, even of unpopular actions such as the war in Iraq. *The Times* and other observers questioned whether these experts were as neutral as their TV reputations would suggest.

Modern broadcasting has blurred the line between truth and fiction with its love of reality TV. Dozens of programmes around the world follow the actions of ordinary people who are thrown into unusual circumstances – locked together in a house, marooned on a desert island or trying to land a part in a major play. Viewers are led to believe that the camera is acting like a fly on the wall, recording human emotions and touching stories as they unfold. Critics argue, however, that some of the action is planned or that the television networks deliberately create rows and arguments to boost the popularity of the programmes.

DEMOCRATIC OR DUMB?

DO YOU THINK THAT REALITY TELEVISION PROGRAMMES ARE A GOOD THING BECAUSE THEY INVOLVE PEOPLE FROM ALL WALKS OF LIFE, AND NOT SIMPLY MEDIA PROFESSIONALS? OR DO THEY REPRESENT THE 'DUMBING DOWN' OF MODERN TELEVISION, FILLING TELEVISION SCREENS WITH POINTLESS ACTIVITIES?

Channels of power

People sometimes refer to crusading broadcasting when they describe how reporters and networks devote themselves to tackling major world problems by making people aware of them. Radio and television have the power to inform and persuade – instantly. *Live Aid,* the massive famine-relief rock concert staged in 1985, came about after the BBC had focused on Ethiopia's hungry population for weeks.

More than 400 million people worldwide watched the live broadcasts of the Live Aid *concerts in 1985, helping to raise $140 million. Top musicians including George Michael, Bono and Paul McCartney played without payment.*

POLITICS ON TELEVISION

British political commentator Andy Mayer, writing on the website openDemocracy in 2002, argued that restrictions on political advertising on British television stifled democracy in the UK. Like some American observers of the British system, he considered these restrictions to be examples of government control. Whereas Americans complain about limiting the amount of political advertising on television, the British see no advertising at all, with the exception of some party political broadcasts during elections. At other times, politics are kept off the screen, according to rules set down by unelected organizations.

Mayer says: 'This puts politics in the same category as dangerous drugs, pornography and tobacco. It infantilizes the British public and in essence suggests that – while we are perfectly capable of reasoning our way through sales promotions for face cream and personal loans – dangerous ideas such as voting Conservative, being nice to whales, or supporting victims of torture should be heavily regulated or in the control of programme makers.'

Television images are also effective tools which persuade people to help by giving money to charities after major disasters such as the 2004 Indian Ocean tsunami, Hurricane Katrina in New Orleans in 2005 or the devastating earthquake in western China in 2008.

A captive audience

Broadcasting power can be harnessed in other ways. Radio and television are excellent media for companies who want to advertise their products. Newspaper readers can turn the page if they do not want to read an advertisement. While TV viewers can change channels when commercials appear on their screens, in fact most televisions stay tuned on the same channel for an entire programme. That means that advertisers have the attention of most of the audience. And if the advertising company is clever, it broadcasts a commercial that is funny or contains a memorable catchphrase or song that people will remember

SPOTLIGHT ON
Powerful messages

Because television and radio can influence the way people think, they have been called upon in times of war. Trying to frighten, persuade or unsettle an enemy by broadcasting propaganda is a tradition going back thousands of years. The ancient Egyptians and Chinese spread rumours about their military might, even before they took on enemies in battle.

Wartime propaganda became widespread during the twentieth century, when broadcasting reached far more people. Both sides used it during the Second World War. British people heard a broadcaster called Lord Haw-Haw calling on them to surrender to the superior forces of Nazi Germany. American soldiers and sailors fighting in the Pacific heard similar messages – also in English – broadcast by a woman called Tokyo Rose. Broadcasting was also important during the Cold War. During this time, the British, American and other governments wanted to send a message of hope to the people of Eastern Europe, whose lives were controlled by communist governments. The BBC World Service, Voice of America, Radio Free Europe and other networks offered them information about life in the freer outside world. East Europeans listened to these radio programmes in secret or faced severe punishments.

British and American radio broadcasts have also given hope to struggling people more recently. Some governments, such as those of Saddam Hussein in Iraq and the Taliban in Afghanistan, control broadcasting in their countries. Programmes from beyond their borders not only offer people a glimpse of the outside world, but also bring them news about what is happening inside their own countries.

and repeat long after the ad has stopped being broadcast. Broadcast advertisements range from 15-second local radio commercials for second-hand car dealers to television commercials running for a minute or longer. The cost of advertising depends on the size of the audience as much as the length of the ad: top-rated TV programmes such as *Coronation Street* or *Big Brother* can charge more than £20,000 for a 30-second advertisement.

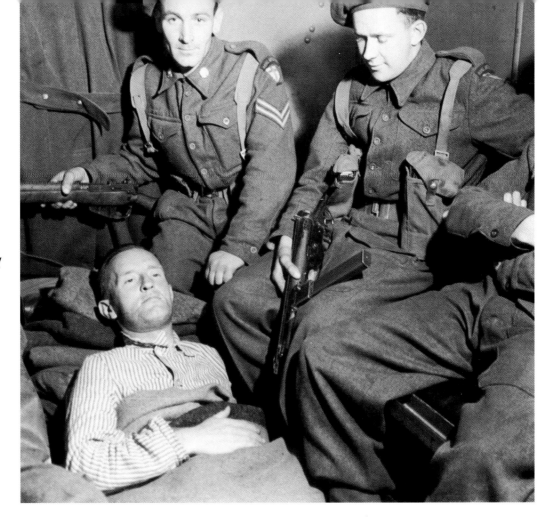

British soldiers guard William Joyce (Lord Haw-Haw), who was captured in Germany at the end of the war. He was later found guilty of treason and executed.

Overall, advertising raises about £4 billion every year for Britain's commercial television stations.

The BBC is one of the few broadcasting networks in the world which prohibits radio and television advertising. The temptation to accept some form of advertising is enormous – money from advertising could save the BBC millions of pounds a year. But such a move would upset most British BBC licence-fee holders, who have been brought up to be proud of the BBC's independence.

Over to YOU

LOFTY IDEALS
THE OFFICIAL MOTTO OF THE BBC IS 'NATION SHALL SPEAK PEACE UNTO NATION'. HOW WELL DO YOU THINK THE ORGANIZATION LIVES UP TO THIS?

Remote control

Everyone agrees that broadcasting is a powerful medium, which can shape people's opinions and change their behaviour. Television, with its combination of images and sound, is particularly equipped to affect viewers. So it is not surprising that many people worry about the effects of watching television and, to a lesser extent, of listening to the radio.

Families have long been aware that most young people would happily spend hours watching the television. Most parents believe that the programmes children watch are not beneficial – lots of loud music and silly shouting, in the opinion of many adults. As a result, households often have rules about how much television children can watch – and

when they watch it. Children might be limited to watching a specific number of hours a day or only be able to watch television when they have finished their homework.

Effects on society

Concerns about broadcasting can be more widespread. Governments in free societies need to recognize these valid worries – about the false reporting of news, about broadcasting power being in the hands of too few people, about advertisers making misleading claims. But at the same time, these societies have a long tradition of free speech. So the job of monitoring broadcasting involves a delicate balancing act.

Broadcasters have often been willing to regulate themselves, reflecting public opinion about what is fit to be broadcast and when. British television networks, for example, observe what is called the nine o'clock watershed. This prevents adult-oriented programmes (with sexual content unsuitable for children, strong language or violence) from being broadcast before nine o'clock in the evening. Television and radio programmers in other countries observe similar limits.

National watchdogs

Most countries have organizations which oversee broadcasting within their borders. These groups often have names which include the words commission, authority or unit and they have wide-ranging responsibilities. At their heart they are intended to act as a link between broadcasters and the public, ensuring fairness, good-quality programming and a chance for listeners and viewers to make complaints.

Britain has long tried to find a balance between national guidance (for fairness, decency and quality) and freedom from outright government control. The BBC was founded to be free of both commercial (business) and government control (see page 18). Commercial radio and television arrived later, so that independent (or non-BBC) broadcasters had separate organizations to act as watchdogs. To make things even more confusing,

Opposite: members of the pop group Hi-5 celebrate the 300th episode of the Australian children's television programme Kids Like Us. *Many parents wonder whether there is any substance behind the fluff and colour of such children's programmes.*

SPOTLIGHT ON
Advertising

Like every other message broadcast on television and radio, advertising can be very powerful – and that power can be misused. TV and radio advertising is monitored closely in every country, and advertisers have to follow strict regulations. Tobacco advertising is banned outright in many countries, and alcohol advertisers must follow strict guidelines (for example, not encouraging young people to drink too much alcohol). Many products are only advertised during the times set aside for adult broadcasting, for example after Britain's nine o'clock watershed.

Children's television programmes – especially those broadcast after school and on Saturday mornings – come under particularly close observation. Young people can be influenced very strongly by advertising. Ofcom and similar organizations in other countries closely monitor advertisements for junk food, violent computer games and other products that children are tempted to buy. In May 2007 Ofcom went further. In an attempt to help children eat more healthily, it banned ads for food high in salt, sugar and fat – key ingredients in junk food.

Alcopops are sold and packaged with bright colours to attract young people. But the makers of these drinks are banned from advertising them on television in many countries.

different types of communications (telephone, television, wireless systems, etc) were also governed by separate organizations.

This complicated system changed in 2003, when the Office of Communications (usually abbreviated to Ofcom) was established, taking over from the various commercial watchdogs. Ofcom looks after competition and fairness in commercial broadcasting: its judgements affect whether private companies receive – and retain – licences to broadcast. It also covers the areas of consumer interest, fairness and some of the legal complications that can develop in the broadcasting industry. Unlike some of the previous watchdogs, Ofcom rulings affect the BBC as well.

Like commercial broadcasters, the BBC has to account for itself to Ofcom, or risk paying large fines. For example, Ofcom fined the BBC £400,000 in July 2008 for running fake phone-in contests on radio and television programmes. Ofcom decided that BBC producers knew that audience members (who had to use expensive phone lines) had no chance of winning these contests, so the broadcasts were ruled unfair.

HIT THE 'OFF' BUTTON?

SOME PEOPLE SAY THAT IF YOU DON'T LIKE WHAT YOU SEE ON TELEVISION (OR HEAR ON THE RADIO), YOU CAN ALWAYS TURN IT OFF OR CHANGE CHANNELS. THEY OFTEN USE THIS ARGUMENT WHEN OTHERS HAVE COMPLAINED ABOUT OFFENSIVE ATTITUDES OR IMAGES BEING BROADCAST. DO YOU THINK THAT THIS 'TURN IT OFF' ARGUMENT IS RIGHT, OR SHOULD BROADCASTING BE SUBJECT TO LIMITS AND CONTROLS?

Becoming part of the picture

Young people can take advantage of rapid changes in broadcasting. The number of radio stations and television channels is increasing, as are ways in which to receive them. People can listen to the radio and watch television on the Internet or even on mobile phones or on screens attached to passenger seats in cars. Large plasma screens showing high-definition television can turn sitting rooms into mini-cinemas.

A teenager videotapes her friends at a skateboarding park. More and more young people are learning skills that can easily be transferred to careers in broadcasting.

SPOTLIGHT ON
DIY broadcasting

Young people interested in broadcasting don't necessarily need to follow official routes to learn more. Mobile phone and video cameras have helped people make their own clips, which can resemble television programmes or even short sections of film. Once again, the Internet offers the opportunity for would-be TV stars and directors to go a step further than they could previously. By uploading clips on to video-sharing websites such as YouTube or social networking sites such as MySpace and Facebook, they can present their work to the world.

While this explosion of choice can confuse adults, young people (who have been used to change all their lives) move easily from one type of broadcasting to another. Computers and the Internet play an increasingly large role in many of these changes, so young people can translate their own computer skills into useful experience.

Major broadcasters such as the BBC and ITV have special sections for young people. Some of the work of Children's BBC (CBBC) and Children's ITV (CITV), for example, simply offers entertainment and educational programmes for young people. But CBBC, like the children's divisions of other broadcasters, also provides a gateway for young people to learn more about radio and television. The CBBC website offers children the chance to learn how their favourite programmes are made – CBBC presenters introduce displays and clips.

Mixed signals

Young people often receive confusing messages about television and radio. Some parents worry about the amount of violence and advertising their children see every day on television. They fear their children will become accustomed to violent scenes or that they will pick up irresponsible attitudes towards junk food or being careful with their money. Other adults claim that the very act of watching television – any television – is physically bad for people. All these hopes and concerns might be less important if we are to believe some

TALKING HEADS

TV HEALTH RISKS?

Dr Aric Sigman is a psychologist who works with and advises the government. He has taken a professional interest in the effects of watching television, and observes: 'The average six-year-old may have already spent more than one full year of their lives in front of a screen. When other screen time is included, the figure is far higher. Children aged 11 to 15 now spend 55 per cent of their waking lives – 53 hours a week, seven and a half hours a day – watching TV and computers, an increase of 40 per cent in a decade. More than half of three-year-olds now have a TV set in their bedrooms.'

Even more worrying are Dr Sigman's conclusions about all this television watching. He is less concerned with criticizing violent TV programmes and films. Instead, he believes that television watching itself can lead to serious health problems. Among these are heart disease, vision problems, becoming overweight and attention difficulties. And those are simply the results of long-term television-watching in childhood. People between the ages of 20 and 60, Dr Sigman argues, could run the risk of contracting Alzheimer's disease because of their television-watching history.

Not everyone agrees with his forecasts, but Dr Sigman has found interested listeners in major newspapers and in the Houses of Parliament.

recent findings about how young people spend their free time. An Ofcom report published in 2006 stated that young people are turning away from traditional media such as television and radio in favour of iPods, mobile phones and online activities. Despite what some parents fear about the dominance of television, young people spend on average one hour less watching television than the population as a whole. They also listen to radio on average for 15 minutes less each day.

Perhaps none of this confusion should be surprising: radio and television have divided opinion ever since they began. Many people link every social change, good or bad, to what we listen to or watch. But perhaps they should ask themselves whether broadcasting has caused these rapid changes or simply reflected them.

HAND IT OVER!

DUNCAN HARPER IS HEADTEACHER OF NEW WOODLANDS PRIMARY SCHOOL IN SOUTH LONDON. NEW WOODLANDS IS UNUSUAL – IT TAKES IN PUPILS WHO HAVE BEEN EXCLUDED FROM NEIGHBOURING PRIMARY SCHOOLS BECAUSE OF THEIR BEHAVIOUR. MR HARPER HAS AN UNUSUAL WAY OF DEALING WITH PUPILS WHO ARE PARTICULARLY BAD-TEMPERED OR TIRED AT HIS SCHOOL – HE TAKES TELEVISIONS FROM THEIR BEDROOMS. IN ORDER TO DO THIS, HE NEEDS THE PERMISSION OF THE PARENTS BUT NOT THE CHILDREN THEMSELVES.

DO YOU THINK HIS APPROACH IS SENSIBLE AND RIGHT, OR IS THIS AN UNFAIR INVASION OF THE CHILDREN'S PRIVACY?

Over to YOU

Glossary

Alzheimer's disease   A mental illness that affects older people's memory and ability to think clearly.

analogue   A broadcasting system that sends out information using a signal that varies.

booster   A device to strengthen a radio or television signal so that it travels further.

broadcast   To send out over the radio or television.

catchphrase   An easy-to-remember slogan.

celebrity   Someone who is often in the news.

Cold War   The years from 1945 to 1990, when the United States and the Soviet Union were constantly on the edge of war with each other.

communist   Someone who believes in a system in which all property is owned by the community and each person contributes and receives according to their ability and needs. A communist government provides work, health care, education and housing, but may deny people certain freedoms.

context   The setting in which something happens.

critic   People who judge artistic productions, usually for newspapers and magazines.

dictator   A person who governs with absolute power.

digital   A broadcasting system that converts information into mathematical symbols before sending it out; the result is a clearer signal because it does not change (as an analogue signal does).

dumbing down   Lowering the standard of something (such as television or radio) so that it is less challenging and educational but more entertaining.

famine   Widespread, prolonged and often deadly hunger in a region.

high-definition television   A digital television system that produces very clear pictures.

mainstream   Popular with most people; not a specialist taste.

mass media   Media that reach the largest number of people.

media   Different forms of communication, including print, radio and television.

media literacy   People's ability to understand and judge broadcast information.

monopoly   Being the only company which sells a product or service. This often allows the company to charge high prices because no other company can compete.

morale   The mental outlook of a group of people, especially when they are facing hardship or war.

multimedia   Involving a combination of media, such as newspapers and television.

party political broadcast   An advertisement for a major political party.

Persians   An Asian nation that had a powerful empire about 3000 years ago.

pornography   Explicit images or programmes that aim to excite people sexually.

prejudice   A negative opinion about an individual or group that is not based on evidence or experience.

propaganda   Information intended to make people think in a certain way, usually ignoring or mocking other points of view.

role model   A successful person who sets an example for others to follow.

satire   Comedy based on poking fun at groups of people or organizations.

scrambled (of a broadcast signal)   Made deliberately hard to receive because a home has not paid for the service.

Second World War   The war from 1939-45 between Germany, Japan, Italy and their allies against the UK, United States, China and their allies.

Soviet Union   The former name of Russia and some of its neighbouring countries, which was a rival of the United States from 1945 to 1990.

tsunami   A massive wave caused by an earthquake on the ocean floor.

watershed   An important dividing line.

Further reading

Is Television a Bad Influence? What Do You Think? series, Kate Shuster (Heinemann Library 2007)

The History of Television, Elizabeth Raum (Heinemann Library 2007)

Television, Careers for the Twenty-First Century series, RT Byrum (Lucent Books 2005)

Radio and Television, Discovering Careers for Your Future series (Facts on File 2005)

Website links

British Academy of Film and Television Arts (BAFTA)

http://www.bafta.org/

CBBC (Children's BBC)

http://www.bbc.co.uk/cbbc/

CITV (Children's ITV)

http://www.citv.co.uk/

Index